The Joy of Their Holiness

The Joy of Their Holiness

Poems by

Peggy Turnbull

Cover design by Shay Culligan

ISBN: 978-1-952326-12-7

Kelsay Books
502 South 1040 East, A-119
American Fork, Utah 94003

For my parents:

Leonard Alden Coombs and Margaret Carlton Coombs

Acknowledgments

I am grateful to the editors of the following journals in which these poems first appeared, some in an earlier form:

Amethyst Review: "After the Funeral Service"
Ancient Paths Online: "God's Language"
Ariel Chart: "Prayer for Petroglyphs"
Door Is A Jar: "Children Who Never Knew Him"
Mad Swirl: "Gift of the Autumn Forest"
Muddy River Poetry Review: "Escarpment"
Nature Writing: "Blueberry"
Pangolin Review: "The Tenderness of an Airport"
Poetry: Alive & Well & Living in Manitowoc! Manitowoc Public
    Library: "Rust Belt Factory"
Poetry Quarterly: "Christmas Bird Count"
Red Eft Review: "Baby Boomer"
Soul-Lit: "When Big Tuba Goes to Heaven"
Verse-Virtual: "Encounter" and "Thanksgiving for City-Dwelling
    Animals"
Wisconsin Poets Calendar: "Buddha in the Auto Zone," "Polka
    Morning Surprise"
Writers Resist: "Kristallnacht, Again," "July Evening, West
    Virginia"
Your Daily Poem: "Final Honors," "When Summer Breathes"

Contents

Blueberry

We brandish vintage juice cans
and pursue you, fellow denizen
of this sandy peninsula. We hunt
like sharks, relentless in our quest
for the glimmer of royal blue
within the verdant scrub.

Once found, we kneel to your level,
fruit-bearing diva of this sun-dappled glen.
We pinch your voluptuous belly
from its umbilical stem, toss you
into the maw of our make-shift pails,
hear your plunk resound in its cavern.

The next morning, we fold you
and your sisters into sticky batter,
drop you by spoonful into a cast iron skillet,
listen to you pop in bacon grease
that sings with heat. After we eat,
we find purple stains
on our white paper plates.

Fabulous fruit, marrow of July,
name of the summer moon,
you are the goddess
of sweet small things,
a thimble full of joy
for any who venture
to find you.

Polka Morning Surprise

Daddy's skin was brown
against his white shirt
his band vest yellow
as a dandelion.
The tuba around his body
a coiled snake that flared
into a hollow head.
Out of its mouth
came sounds
round as bubbles
that danced
into my attic room.
On Sunday mornings
we kids ran downstairs
to see his silver tuba
at rest on the carpet.
Sometimes
thin slices of wedding cake
wrapped in fancy napkins
lay beneath its gleaming bell.
Daddy's gift, carried back
from some northern dance hall,
where a bride in a white dress
told him, here's some for your children,
take it home.

Baby Boomer

My father played music on Saturday nights, slept late
on Sundays. We banged in after church, returned
to a kitchen of Holy Land scents, briny olives,
zingy red sauce that snuggled into al dente pasta,

the kitchen a strange riot after days of meat loaf
and fish sticks. Dad poured himself a glass of cold amber,
foamy enough to make a fake mustache with, though
we never did, not after tasting the bitter stuff.

We lunched with the TV on. Romy Gosz trumpeted
to a dance floor filled with locals in their Sunday best,
promenading to polkas and waltzes.
Some couples never stopped twirling. Mostly men

with women, sometimes two women. There weren't
enough men to go around, I decided. At our house,
we knew not all had made it home, the jolly music
always in the way when we asked to find out more.

Children Who Never Met Him

saw the soldier smile
in a picture frame
at grandma's.

Ran in his back yard
on brittle grass
avoiding shadows.

Sometimes they looked up—

felt an angel hover
during kickball
or jumping rope—

no one was ever there.

Kristallnacht, Again

In Indiana, empty-headed cornstalks wave
at the interstate. Peeling wooden crosses
lurk among the goldenrod, forgotten.

Deployed decades ago with evangelical zeal,
they decorated Appalachian highways when
my friend Daniel still lived in West Virginia.

They unleashed his crystal nightmares of Vienna.
He knocked at our screen door, asked,
If they come again, will you hide me?

July Evening, West Virginia

I gather stunted apples
from the garden
peel them, carve out
their bruised flesh
put them to simmer
with cinnamon

On the radio
a woman's voice
recollects the death
of a famous poet
how his friends
sat on the floor for hours
attending the old Buddhist
as he slowly let go

I don't have time to meditate
A child needs me
I stir the pan
certain he will love
whatever I find good

The poet at last surrendered
left his queer poems
to the living
for queer children
to someday find
and gain strength
from the joy of their holiness

We eat and go outside
watch fireflies blink
as the darkness grows

Buddha in the AutoZone

He wears inner peace like an old Saturday shirt
perfect for the first chilly day in October,
faded from washing, but long-sleeved and cozy,
so comfortable that even in the AutoZone checkout line
he smiles like Buddha. Across the street,

children dart, half-hidden by a flickering screen
of falling birch leaves. Families parade past, stroll
to the central square where red-green-gold apples fill
tables and white paper sacks. A farmer laments
the rainy growing season and offers a slice

of Ginger Gold. When I was young, I never saw
tawny dreadlocks or caramel-colored skin
like that of the man with the beatific smile.
I hug my bag of apples, grateful for the day's soft
edges, the blessings in my tiny, mortal life.

Encounter

On Halloween Day,
led astray by a path
hidden under oak leaves,
a puzzled hiker stands
among a herd of deer who stare,
reproachfully, at the stranger
invading their terrain.

She begs their pardon,
"I'm lost!" Two wild turkeys
strut toward a broken fence.
She follows, the view opens
to rusty hills across the canyon.
Quiet as decay she sits,
blends into the earth.

The pigeon-colored sky
inexplicably asks
for her prayer. She adores
the beauty here, it scours
her being. A wish wells
within. The desire she's carried
for years leaks out.

And it rings. A vision
of wrecked lives spins.
A fizzled balloon.

She follows trail blazes
to leave, soon loses her way
again, the unspoken prayer
an awkward burden to hump out.
She stumbles among unfamiliar trees.
The deer stay out of sight.

The First

We sleep in a canyon on a rock bed.
When he leaves me at morning,
I watch the boulders of his joints
tumble and drag.

Alone, I birth soil and slime.
He presses his feet into the planet.
Wherever he wanders, water rushes
to fill the void. Our reunions
echo like asteroids colliding.
We know no other language.

I begin to sprout trees from my head.
My feet petrify into minerals.
He also settles, his gangly arms
stiffen and slow. Our children—
saplings, stones, waterfalls—
journey to their own countries.

One evening he does not return
and I cannot free myself to find him.
As I struggle with my tethers, desire
makes my arms reach and stretch
until I grasp the world in an embrace,
weeping. He is *He* no more, but remains
somewhere inside my love.

Prayer for Petroglyphs

Who looks at peckings on the face of rocks
still visible, though from an ancient hand,
and is not stirred to wonder at intent,
of whom was meant to read these marks?

Man-shapes and spirals glow in evening rays,
when shadows lengthen in-between cliff's clefts,
on boulders pink and brown as desert sand,
above saguaro and the prickly pear.

Perhaps Hohokam simply told the tale
of where they found their game one hunting trip.
Perhaps their people worshiped here at times,
gave thanks for changing seasons and for meat.

Their poems remain, preserved in air.
Aggressive bees, protect these mysteries.

Escarpment

The April forest teeters
on a limestone ledge
thick with fallow saplings.

Trills and chirrups echo.
Yellow warblers, song sparrows
flitter among dolomite outcrops,

the pocked remains
of a prehistoric coral reef
once alive in a Silurian sea

until it receded,
and glaciers flattened land
older than the Appalachians.

The birds' chatter ceases.
Their hush feels watchful,
the species alert to us.

If I could pirouette for them
in hiking boots, I would.
Instead I contemplate eons,

the cataclysms that made this location,
then envision epochs forward,
climate altered,

temperate forest tropical,
flamingos wading in warm water,
or some new genus

evolved from chaos.
And I fail.

Gravity holds us
to the surface of a rock
that spins in a vast void.
Nothing we know will last.

We are here today
to sing our one song.
Like the birds.

Christmas Bird Count

We drive on country roads in the quiet
of a long drizzle. Burst of seven starlings.

Out of the mist comes a man shuffling across
a blue lake smooth as ceramic. He scuffs

small splashes of water on top of the ice. Bob
scans the shore with binoculars, brings back a whiff

of wood-smoke. He counts eleven pigeons I don't see.
A crow investigates a lawn in Golf Course Estates.

Six geese fly over a barnyard. Sheep rest
in a small enclosure, some wearing canvas jackets.

Lambs scamper toward us as we slow to greet them.
My body grows beyond its borders into the moment

of their attention. *Yes, I see you. Yes, we are connected.*
Thank you for looking at my face. Three crows peck

in mud and stubble. I stare longingly at dark circles
in the trees, left-behind leaves clinging to bare branches.

I will them to move, reveal wings, fly.
A red-tailed hawk lights on a post nearby.

Thanksgiving for City-Dwelling Creatures

Creator, thank you for mammals
that share our neighborhoods.

For the coyote who leaps onto my path.
His fur gleams white in my headlights.
Keep him unhurt, that he may continue
to range across acres of farmland
and raid furrowed fields.

For the fawn with spindle-legs
who swims across a dark river,
scrambles up a steep bank,
and fades into a backyard wood.

For sightings on city walks:
skunk, muskrat, mink, fox, possum.
Like disguised fairy folk, they appear,
then vanish into concealed worlds.

May we maintain sufficient habitat
for them in our tame neighborhoods.

May they pursue their restless hungers
safe from poisons, pellets, and killing traps.

May these wild beings remind us
that we are not alone, remind us
of your vast and mysterious presence.

Creator, help us coexist.

Gift of the Autumn Forest

a cub-sized lump
    slumps against
        dark asphalt

magenta slit
    in blue-black fur—
        a goner

six crows make
    a hexagonal shape
        around him

obsidian feathers
    like priestly garb
        at this fresh altar

birches release
    yellow leaves—
        glitter from a silver sky

falls on land old as myth
    blesses the greedy
        with death's largesse

The Tenderness of an Airport

An old man struggles out of the transport van,
finds the ledge too narrow, the gap too steep.
I place my hand under the stranger's arm,
then his elbow, the way I touch my aged mother.

Helpfully. Like a nurse. The man pauses
at the airline entrance, says, "thank you,"
and smiles with such warmth I think about it
for days as I trek to pyramids underneath

Mexico's blue skies. Pilgrims dressed in white
walk cobblestoned streets with me. They lift
their palms to the sun in Teotihuacan
to receive its energy. Even airports absorb

the emotion of departures and arrivals. Within
the concrete, love waits like a crocus in March.

After the Funeral Service

Long-haired men lift the casket,
carry it
through the church's double doors.

The congregation sings, "Onward,
Christian Soldiers."
A vibration begins in my throat.

I think I hear a bat navigating
the rafters,
echolocating while waves of sound

surround it and the coffin.
Melody travels
where we cannot. Its frequencies

intersect with dusty corners,
shadows.
We sing to our beloved lost one.

The martial meter of the familiar hymn
a heartbeat
for the journey to our Creator. I sing

with spirit. We all do, as if we think
our voices
can pierce the membrane between

the living and the dead.
We sing loudly,
as if there is no doubt.

When Summer Breathes

Because we waste not, when gooseberries
dangle from our fence, I harvest the sour spheres,
eager to can. My husband toils alone inside,
ticks numbers off a spreadsheet. Our child

skips in circles, gyrates to peepers bellowing
in the violet evening. I tell him fairies dance
between the roots of our ancient pine. I want
to give him a world suffused with awe.

We travel to old growth forests, waterfalls
and rivers, seek the magic of summer hail,
the loon's cry. For a trace of time we are earth's
acolytes, tending to tomatoes, savoring pears.

Come out, Dad, our son shrieks. We hear a chair
scrape against the bare floor, the screen door squeak.
The night ratchets up in happiness. And creation,
bringer of our abundance—how to bless it in return?

Final Honors

I stand for hours, chatting with strangers
who extol my husband's deceased dad.
My emotions well, but I stay stalwart
to honor him, that old Marine.

The funeral director drapes
an American flag on the casket.
His grandsons carry it to the hearse
for its trip to their grandmother,
who waits for her husband to enter
the newly shoveled emptiness beside her.

An honor guard of two stands ready
to perform their staccato ritual.
With white gloves they give a slow-motion salute,
crease and fold our country's flag.

A solemn "Taps" wafts. July's mid-day light
vibrates around the bugler, who stands on a mound
and glows like a heavenly messenger
arrived from the past, from before we were born.

I flash. These characters
from his life's earliest chapters appear
again at its end to claim him,
while we, his family, sit at graveside, bereft.

The funeral director lifts a spade of dirt,
drops it in. A Marine bends on one knee,
offers my husband the flag.
My cheeks feel suddenly wet.

Rust Belt Factory

After John Boyle O'Reilly: "Cry of the Dreamer"

I was tired of broken windows
at the abandoned factory,
weary of shards in the shadows,
that puncture tires in the street.
And I yearned for the days of my father,
when the factory lines were long.
For workers made this town stronger,
made dreams that carried on.

I was tired of millionaires buying,
and buying and selling again.
Deboning the factory of value,
leaving asbestos and lead.
Removing its pipes for the copper,
prying its timbers away.
What used to be vibrant, now fodder
for fires, vandals, decay.

I was happy the city was willing
to pay to get rid of the blight.
Four walls, seven stories of building
collapsed into dust at the site,
made oceans of rubble and concrete,
small mountains of yellow bricks.
A painful wound deleted
from the central city's breast.

The site stands fenced and vacant.
Sea gulls peck in its dirt.
There's only a concrete doorframe
where Steelworkers entered and left.
Their history preserved in that doorframe,
their legend forever impressed.
Their toil made this town stronger.
We need dreamers to progress.

When Big Tuba Goes to Heaven

God, don't let silence rule the hereafter.
Our father's nonagenarian lungs
are a testament to his handle
from C.B. radio days: Big Tuba.

Let paradise be a place where he can play
polkas at a perpetual party. Once a night
he'll sing *The Blue Skirt Waltz* in Bohemian.
The crowd will hush and strain to hear words

their parents spoke in the language of childhood.
Between songs, musicians will wet their whistles
from a bottle hidden in a paper sack,
discreetly passed. Let him wear a cap

for the Chicken Dance with a barnyard animal
glued on it, complete with plastic droppings
attached to the bill. If kingdom come
is fit for the jocund, please hold your horses.

He'll tell you when he's ready
and there will be nothing quiet,
nothing tame, nothing solemn—

just his thunderous *alleluias*
piercing the pink glory of the promised land
as you welcome Big Tuba home.

About God's Language

After dinner, the adults chat.
I don't know what they discuss.
Their children make demands of me—
    Bring seven shells down from the shelf
        so they can discuss what they see.
    Pour water on Petoskey stones
        to reveal the honeycomb patterns.
    Print pages for them to color—
        a unicorn and a mandala.

They find a yoga mat in a dusty corner,
unfurl it to serve as their station.
I leave them on the floor coloring.
The house settles around them,
their room glows with electric light.
Whenever the adults pause,
I hear the children's soft syllables,
fragments of their songs.

With voices as beautiful as the Gospel,
they speak to themselves and to each other.
The world could rejoice in this language,
easily:
    Make all children fed, sheltered, loved—
        and listen.

About the Author

Peggy Turnbull lives in Manitowoc, Wisconsin, the place of her birth. Now retired, she is a former college librarian who spent most of her career in southern West Virginia. She won The Mill Prize for Poetry in 2019 and her poem, "About God's Language," was nominated for the Pushcart Prize. She sings in a community chorale and enjoys exploring local parks and trails, especially those on the Lake Michigan coast. Peggy's micro-chapbook, *Rocking Chair Abstract,* was published by the Origami Poems Project. She is a member of the Wisconsin Fellowship of Poets, the Wisconsin Library Association, and St. James Episcopal Church.

Made in the USA
Monee, IL
28 July 2020